Find Who You Are t

CW01081595

Raising Your

Rare Personality

Discover Your Personality and What Makes You Rare. Learn How You Relate and Contrast Yourself to Others. Increase Resilience, Reduce Crisis, and Unlock Your Ideal Career

Clear Career Inclusive Series - Book 1

Devi Sunny

GRAB YOUR GIFT

You can download your free **Personality Strength Report** at www.clearcareer.in to understand your personality type, unique cognitive functions, and integrated personality growth path.

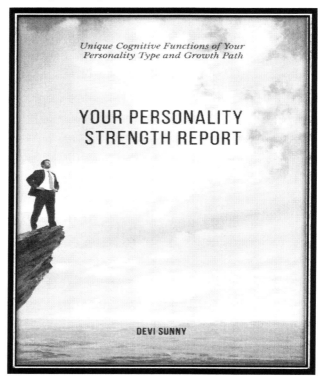

Contents

Clear Career Inclusive Series

1) Book 1

   Raising Your Rare Personality

   Discover Your Personality and What Makes You Rare. Learn How You Relate and Contrast Yourself to Others. Increase Resilience, Reduce Crisis, and Unlock Your Ideal Career.

2) Book 2

   Upgrade as Futuristic Empaths

   5 Steps to Build the Profile of Intuitive Feelers for Successful Careers and to Develop Empathy as Strength. An Empath's Guide to Existential Crisis, Finding Purpose & Clarity in Chaos.

3) Book 3

   Onboard as Inclusive Leaders

   Increase Job Readiness; Improve Performance & Innovation, and Profit by Learning Inclusive Leadership Skills. Identify Unconscious Biases, Ensure Psychological Safety & Better Workplace Productivity.

Upcoming Books are from the Series: **Fearless Empathy**

About the Book

Why are people different? Why do some of us behave in a certain way? Why are we influenced by certain people, prefer certain jobs, and are driven by certain ideas? Why do we get along well in some situations, while resisting some other situations? Are there people who generally behave like us, who share the same patterns of response, and face similar problems? MBTI answers all these questions. Myers-Briggs Type Indicator (MBTI), a tool to identify personality typology, classifies people into 16 types. We all fall into one of these 16 personality types based on our psychological preferences.

Our aptitudes are innate and our interests are acquired. But our personality is both inherited (natural) and nurtured (developed). Many of us are unaware of our natural preferences and therefore struggle with existential crisis and career crisis, leading to many uncertain situations. Awareness of our psychological preferences helps us take better control of situations in our life and work. This understanding will largely ease the expectation levels we have about ourselves and of others. Also, knowing who we are, make us wise and helps us make more informed decisions in our life and career.

Some personality types are classified as rare personalities as per MBTI. Because they are not common among the majority of the people we meet, these types have a high chance of feeling misunderstood, as they appear vastly different from the majority of personality types. Knowing that they do not 'fit' into any specific category will cause unnecessary confusion and pain in them, and they struggle to get along with the majority without knowing that they are in a class of their own.

Every personality type can grow only when they know their natural preferences, their strengths, and weaknesses. To play with their strengths and to improve upon their weakness is a decision each should take at one point or the other. Eventually, it leads to a better version of their types and that transformation has the capacity of making an impact, however small, in the world around us.

This book is intended to make the reader understand about rare personality types. An effort is made to assist you with insights on why some people are different among us. Along with all other types and the rare types, the rarest personality type INFJ growth and INFJ Careers are explored in detail.

The author is sharing her experience as an INFJ, Advocate or Counsellor type and this book is to bring solidarity to who they are. INTP, INTJ, ENFJ, ENTJ, and ENTP are some of the types that are also rare when compared to other common types.

The rarer your personality is, the more your chances of struggling to come to terms with the world around you.

This book is also an opportunity to further explore suitable careers for all MBTI types, especially for rare personality types. The method of identifying and developing any MBTI type is explained by taking examples of suitable INFJ jobs, work styles, and career paths.

All in all, this book is intended to show how the understanding of various personality types is essential in having a more meaningful life. The information in this book will help in developing all the personality types and their respective cognitive functions, as well as developing empathy or logic, which is essential for holistic development. This will help them make appropriate decisions in life and achieve success in their career.

"One does not always do the best there is.

One does the best one can"

Catherine the Great

Introduction

"No one on any plane of existence is infallible or knows everything we need to know"

-Shepherd Hoodwin

In her book '**Gifts Differing**', **Isabel Briggs Myers** quotes, *"The Less frequent types find their infrequency an obstacle to their development"*.

- **Who is a 'Less Frequent' personality type?**
- **Why are some of us called 'Rare Personalities'?**
- **How do we energize ourselves and choose our lifestyle?**
- **How do we process information and make decisions?**

When we think about personalities, many people come across in our minds. Most of these personalities are famous for having achieved something monumental in their life.

We all have a personality that defines us at any point of time, ironically this personality also gives rise to strange reactions during stress. Welcome to the world of contradictions! Most of us can recall well- known public figures who have destructive personalities. So why do some people behave in a destructive way while others are able to leave memorable imprints in history?

In his book, '**Thinking Fast and Slow**', **Daniel Kahneman** quotes, *"The statement 'Hitler loved dogs and little children' is shocking no matter how many times you hear it because any trace of kindness in someone so evil violates the expectations set up by the halo effect".*

As the person who orchestrated World War II and the Holocaust, which led to the death of at least 40 million people, Hitler was reportedly a teetotaler, a non-smoker, and a vegetarian; so was Mahatma Gandhi. Interestingly, both are the same personality type. So, what brought about the difference in their persona? Are there any differences in the underlying cognitive functions that manifest their actions?

Before diving deep into the MBTI Personality types, specifically the rare personality types, I want to share with you the instances which led me to find myself as an INFJ. I cannot recall when I commenced my journey of self-exploration however, I observed my behavior after activating WhatsApp in 2016. From being a laggard in joining the popular instant messaging application, I became within a short time, the most active member in most of my chat groups.

In the smaller groups, I found myself a channel to express my thoughts freely and was successfully able to generate great enthusiasm for myself and my lot of online buddies. I joined in sharing memes, trolls, stickers besides the well-forwarded jokes, and found myself with a wider grin on my face with each passing day.

I found immense satisfaction in penning lengthy messages, sharing inspirational videos, and engaging my pals in meaning-laden philosophies. Along with the satisfaction of adding value & fun, there was a nagging thought if I was acting weird while also feeling overwhelmed at times.

It was strange, that I was involved well over what was normal as compared to others in wanting to keep up the spirits and morale of the people in groups. I noticed that I was trying to keep the debates and conflicts in chat groups at arm's length. To my surprise, I found myself in as a protector to keep the harmony and ensure justice at times. I was brutally honest, when the need arose. I lent my shoulder and my ear to my forlorn and tearful cronies.

I admit it did cross my mind that my people-pleasing persona could perhaps be perceived as an intentional goodwill- building tactic, but that did not stop me, because I thought it was the right thing to do. I was always an odd one.

Though I enjoyed myself to the fullest on the online groups, I started second-guessing my online presence when I found myself as the only one to respond first and wondered how group members could ignore birthdays and achievements shared in these groups. I guess I couldn't ignore such joyful occasions possibly due to the grains of empathy and compassion bespeckled in my personality. With time, I developed a resentment towards the lack of reciprocation and empathy by the less-than-considerate members in the group.

I questioned the idea of instant gratification drawn through such social interactions. I continuously mulled over making a change in direction on a professional front, however, my online overindulgence made sure I was slow to achieve that goal. As a start to a remedy, I was glued to my mobile in the quest for videos on digital detoxification.

I knew that in order to stick to my decision for a career change, I had to translate the seriousness of my intent into action. The effort to pull out from online groups to focus on work thus started. I contemplated several times and did exit my key online groups. While most of my friends granted me my space, some kept constantly adding me back to the group on account of the freedom friendship brought.

Back in the group, I was into everything that gave caution to concerns of the future. Sharing content on Naturopathy, healthy living, were some such contents that were close to my heart.

I gave blunt opinions and was constantly advocating for environmental degradation and climate change. One topic thread led to the other and very soon heated discussions like capitalism versus socialism also cropped up. Ironically, I am a naturally conflict-averse person. I believe most times I have admitted leniency for being one among the fairer sex and thus escaped the harsher counters from my male group-mates.

However, there were episodes where confrontations were head-on at full steam.

I exited several times after being repeatedly added to the group and blamed myself for my inconsistency. I was also sensing a vulnerability because I was constantly responding to forwards and posts and so I felt the need to modulate my intensity.

During this online river rafting experience, I locked career counseling as my new career move. This decision was in alignment with my work experience and my constant urge for updating my groups with, available courses and future jobs opportunities. I always felt the import that information that benefitted anyone should definitely be shared.

Being an ex-sustainability consultant by profession (once my dream role), I was still searching for a deeper purpose in life and the cherry on the cake would be if I could exercise a good amount of independence in my work.

As my career counseling training progressed, I explored psychometric tests and personality types.

I sat through the MBTI Personality type test and the results stunned me as it justified my observations about my behaviors and inclinations. It was a relief to know that my Myers and Briggs personality test results were pleasantly very much on the charts and that I was one among the 'normal' but rare personality types that walked the Earth. I went ahead and shared the tests within my circle which resonated with my excitement and self-exploration.

I envisioned reaching out to a wider audience, to share the happiness of self-discovery, through which people could work with their Cognitive Functions towards building ideal careers and meaningful relationships.

By this book, I intend to bring an understanding of the different personality types, especially the rare types and familiarize these types of persons to the readers.

It will bring ease of understanding of the different mindsets and will help to approach life with the least resistance and unobstructed flow.

Also, the career preferences for each personality type are prescribed as a reference in order to take suitable timely decisions according to the respective type.

The World Economic Forum, in its post on the 3 skillsets for the workers of 2030, referring to the report from Mckinsey Global Institute, predicts a dramatic increase in the demand for employee hours across 3 skills namely, Higher Cognitive, Social & Emotional, and Technological Skills.

The faster we adapt, the better our chances are to survive the changes in the world. Improvement is a constant upgrade of ourselves from the baseline of where we stand today.

At no point in time, is our knowledge complete. The deeper we are aware of our inner self and the external opportunities available, the greater the chances for our personal as well as professional growth. Personal transformation foreruns professional growth.

Enjoy the upcoming chapters as we dive into a fascinating journey of personalities, and use this understanding to help each other upgrade and win a fulfilling career.

1. MBTI Personality Types

"It is up to each person to recognize his or her true preferences"-Isabel Briggs Myers

MBTI (Myers Briggs Type Indicator) Personality Types

The 16 personalities identified under the MBTI Personality type tests are internationally used by counseling psychologists to assess the personality of a person. The first book on MBTI was published in 1944 by a mother-daughter duo Myers & Briggs, and the concepts are originally derived from Carl Jung's theory of psychological types.

Even though the validity of this theory and test is not completely accepted by many scientists, it's undoubtedly one of the most popular personality tests. They are used in personal development programs, relationship guidance, and career suggestions.

What is your personality type according to MBTI?

Before understanding your personality type, it is important to realize why you should know about your personality type.

Unpredictable reactions, either ours or of others, in our personal & professional lives usually lead to unnecessary stress and confusion. Unawareness about personality types sometimes leads to bigger problems which cost both peace of mind, time, and money. Many mishaps have been caused due to the lack of knowledge, which could have been avoided with the presence of mind and timely information. Though knowledge about varied personalities may not help to change people, it helps us understand the weaknesses and strengths associated with any type. It also helps to find blind spots and make personality improvements.

Knowledge of one's personality helps one make informed decisions, which will reduce the chances of careers misfits, strained relationships, and complex social interactions.

It brings about an understanding of a person's general tendencies, interests, reactions, and casual behavior.

More interesting is the fact that we share our personality types with others who process information and behave in a fashion similar to ours in any given circumstances.

This information is relieving and reassuring, as it opposes the general belief that we are to be held responsible for our reaction. It leads to a better understanding of people and their behavior and can ease our expectations of others and helps us to adjust to issues on a personal and professional level.

It is a relief for anyone to know that they belong to a personality type with similar thought processes. This leads to an increase in their acceptance by others especially when they work on their weakness and utilize their strengths.

MBTI Theory tells us in detail how a person will behave in a normal or a stressed environment and what their cognitive functions are.

This information can be used for the holistic growth of one's personality benefitting ourselves and those around us. My transformation into a career consultant is one of the recommended careers for my personality type and hence my current career direction is an amalgamation of my interest, strength, and aptitude. As this is an opportunity for me to serve society with information, it has become my ideal career or my IKIGAI (life purpose).

How do we understand our personality type by using the MBTI Test?

MBTI test examines people for their leading behaviors according to their preferences, energizing traits (Introversion/Extroversion), Information processing (Intuition/Sensory), decision making based on feeling and thinking (Feeler/Thinker), and their lifestyle preferences (Judging/Perceiving). The test gives a combination of a 4-letter abbreviation, in my case INFJ, based on my prominent style of behavior.

INFJ reveals that Introverted, Intuitive, Feeler, and Judging patterns are prominent in my personality compared to other functions.

This test is a measure of the percentage of these natural preferences based on our response to a set of probing questions formulated for this purpose. The general inclination for each type is different and the personality types are classified according to the combinations of most likely preferences for each criterion.

MBTI personality classification is based on the below criteria:

MBTI Type Identification Chart – Criteria and Corresponding Inclination

Criteria	Energizing	Information Processing	Decision Making	Lifestyle
Type	E-Extrovert	S-Sensing	T-Thinking	P-Perceiving
Inclination	Outgoing	Factual	Logical	Spontaneous
Type	I-Introvert	N-Intuitive	F-Feeling	J-Judging
Inclination	Inward	Possibilities	Emotional	Planned

There can be 16 personality types possible from the above combinations as shown below. Free online tests are available to determine your personality type which is shared in the Resources section.

You can take the test to understand your personality type from 16personalities.com and here you can understand better what every 4-letter acronym stands for and which category they belong.

MBTI 16 Personality Types			
Analysts			
INTJ	INTP	ENTJ	ENTP
Diplomats			
INFJ	INFP	ENFJ	ENFP
Sentinels			
ISTJ	ISFJ	ESTJ	ESFJ
Explorers			
ISTP	ISFP	ESTP	ESFP

When we observe people in our social circles, we can make out the type they belong to by the way they behave. Though taking the test will help find the personality type of people accurately, we can also read their types without them taking the tests.

We will see the type preferences in detail as below:

Introversion/Extroversion (I / E)

These are two approaches people use to energize themselves. Introverts have a high inclination to draw their energy from introspection and silence. Extroverts on the other hand gather inspiration from interacting with people. Extroverts prefer multiple circles of friends, thrive in social gatherings, are prone to take initiative, are talkative, and are enthusiasts by nature. Introverts keep to themselves and so have very few friends, however, they are good listeners and are mostly independent.

Intuition / Sensory (N / S)

These preferences are understood based on how people receive & process information.

Intuitive people conclude from the perspectives they have developed in their minds, whereas people who use sensory stimulation uses sensory inferences to process information.

If intuitive people are future-oriented, the Sensing type has more access to current details and acts faster than the intuitive type, who will be considering possibilities and are normally idealists.

Feeler / Thinker (F / T)

Feelers and Thinkers can be classified based on how they make decisions. Thinkers are more logical and they consider facts in decision making. But Feelers prefer emotions over logic to make decisions. Thinking types are firmer and more impersonal. Their decisions are objective-based. The Feelers are more passionate and empathic, who prefer to avoid criticism and conflicts.

Judging / Perceiving (J / P)

Judgers and Perceivers are classified based on their lifestyles.

Judgers are more organized and decisive who like fast action. They are inflexible and are less ready to cope with the unexpected. Perceivers are more spontaneous.

They are more open to opportunities and their approach is more flexible. They are less likely to follow a schedule and hence there are chances of deviating from objectives.

In a nutshell, these are natural preferences based on the most likely actions of individuals and they may have to work towards improving the other preferences. These preferences help in understanding areas of strengths and weakness considering the qualities of each personality type.

According to the MBTI Manual, Published by CPP, The Personality type distribution in the general population is as below:

MBTI Type	Frequency In Population (%)
ISFJ	13.8
ESFJ	12.3
ISTJ	11.6
ISFP	8.8
ESTJ	8.7
ESFP	8.5
ENFP	8.1
ISTP	5.4
INFP	4.4
ESTP	4.3
INTP	3.3
ENTP	3.2
ENFJ	2.5
INTJ	2.1
ENTJ	1.8
INFJ	1.5

Chapter Summary

1.   MBTI is a personality type classification developed by Myers & Briggs. It classifies people into 16 types.

2.   Understanding the personality types makes efficient co-existence in the workplace, family, and relationships.

3.   Awareness of personality types will give us better control and personal growth opportunities.

2. MBTI Cognitive Functions

Darkness cannot drive out darkness; only light can do that. Hate cannot drive out hate; only love can do that"

Martin Luther King Jr.

We often label people we meet as nice, mean, easy to get along with etc, based on their behavior towards us. Consider a situation where 'X' is always behaving in an irritating manner towards 'Y'. This leads to 'Y' labelling 'X' as irritating. Also, in the picture is 'Z' who is very pleasantly mannered towards 'Y'.

Now consider multiple groups consisting of 'X', 'Y' and 'Z''s in the world, who have similar behavior. It should ideally increase the understanding level of 'Y', considering the fact that that behaviour from X was not specific to Y, but that is how all X behave towards all the Y's. As is the case with the behaviour of all Z towards all Y's. Here, X, Y, and Z belong to different personality types. What makes them different from each other is their behavioural patterns based on their cognitive functions, which are unique and separate in the normal environment and in the stressed environment for all the 16 personality types.

The Cognitive Function and its importance to a personality:

The Cognitive Functions of any personality are defined by their mental abilities like learning, thinking, reasoning, remembering, problem-solving, decision making, and attention. Primary functions are our natural way of reacting to any situation. Shadow functions are an unconscious part of our personality. The shadow appears when our dominant Primary functions are having a hard time solving a problem or coping with stress.

Primary Functions include the Leading Function which is the most mature, followed by Assisting-Supporting Function, Relief (Slightly Developed Function), and Ambitious (Least Developed Function). Shadow functions include Opposing, Cynical, Deceiving, and Immobilizing functions in the order based on their dominance in respective personality types. When a personality puts the Primary functions into play, the situation he/she is in appears to be healthy, whereas, in an unhealthy situation, the personality uses their shadow cognitive functions in an unpredictable and distorted manner. It is usually an unconscious behavior on the part of the respective personality type. These cognitive functions help us to group personalities based on the functions they tend to use the most.

The resulting function types include:

Introverted Intuition (**Ni**), Extroverted Intuition (**Ne**), Introverted Sensing (**Si**), Extroverted Sensing (**Se**), Introverted Thinking (**Ti**), Extroverted Thinking (**Te**), Introverted Feeling (**Fi**), Extroverted Feeling (**Fe**), etc.

The abbreviations for these function types are chosen from the type names themselves. For eg, the 'N' from Intuition and 'I' from Introverted together form 'Ni' which represent Introverted Intuition and so forth.

Let us review the role of the 8 cognitive functions in the table below:

Function	Roles
Ni	Knowing, Perspectives
Ne	Creating, Exploration
Si	Preserving, Memory
Se	Doing, Sensation
Ti	Reasoning, Accuracy
Te	Systemizing, Effectiveness
Fi	Valuing, Authenticity
Fe	Connecting, Harmony

One can take the MBTI personality test to reveal their 4-letter personality type and understand the corresponding cognitive functions- Primary and Shadow functions.

Cognitive Primary Functions of MBTI Personality Types

The primary cognitive functions of the 16 personalities are unique to each type. Hence at any point in time, with any person, one in the 16 combinations of these cognitive functions is the predicted behavior according to their personality type.

Cognitive Functions are categorized as 'Judging' based on how people decide action and as 'Perceiving' based on how people intake information. Thinking & Feeling functions are Judging functions (J) and Intuitive & Sensing Functions are Perceiving Functions(P). The second and third letters of the 4-letter acronym of any personality type are called Functional Pair (PJ), which is a Judging Function and a Perceiving function. For Example, For INFJ, The Functional Pair is 'NF'. The Judging Function is F and Perceiving Function is N.

The cognitive functions are a combination of 4 functions, called the functional stack. It is represented in a JPPJ or a PJJP Format. Based on the fourth letter of any personality type (J or P), the first extroverted function of any personality type is decided from the Functional Pair.

In an introverted personality type, it is represented by the "i,e,i,e" ('introverted, extroverted, introverted, extroverted') format, and in an extroverted personality type, it is represented by the "e,i,e,i" ('extroverted, introverted, extroverted, introverted') format.

For Example, For Introverted Judging Types, the functional Stack is in i,e,i,e format and PJJP format. For Introverted Perceiving types, the functional Stack is in a i,e,i,e format and JPPJ format. For Extroverted Judging types, the functional Stack is in e,i,e,i format and PJJP format. For Extroverted Perceiving types, the functional Stack is in e,i,e,i format and JPPJ format.

The below table indicates the primary cognitive function of the 16 personality types. Since the type formation comes naturally to any personality type, it will be their most predicted behavior.

Type	Leading	Assistant	Relief	Ambitious
		Primary Cognitive Functions		
ISTJ	Si	Te	Fi	Ne
ISFJ	Si	Fe	Ti	Ne
INFJ	Ni	Fe	Ti	Se
INTJ	Ni	Te	Fi	Se
ISTP	Ti	Se	Ni	Fe
ISFP	Fi	Se	Ni	Te
INFP	Fi	Ne	Si	Te
INTP	Ti	Ne	Si	Fe
ESTP	Se	Ti	Fe	Ni
ESFP	Se	Fi	Te	Ni
ENFP	Ne	Fi	Te	Si
ENTP	Ne	Ti	Fe	Si
ESTJ	Te	Si	Ne	Fi
ESFJ	Fe	Si	Ne	Ti
ENFJ	Fe	Ni	Se	Ti
ENTJ	Te	Ni	Se	Fi

The behavior of the cognitive primary function in personality types:

Introverted Intuition (Ni)

The Introverted Intuition function makes a personality type extremely aware of the interconnectedness of actions in the world and their future implications. This function makes people highly aware of situations waiting to happen, before their actual occurrence; envisaging patterns, possibilities, and impacts on the future. Their thoughts are so interweaved that with one real event happening, they unconsciously get insights which lead to "Aha" moments for them. They can draw patterns from the information received and usually caution those around them of forthcoming situations and convince them to change their course of action.

Extroverted Intuition (Ne)

Extroverted Intuition helps people ideate and discern multiple possibilities by connecting the events and actions of people. The optimistic, curious, and creative side of this function type provides leverage, to outsmart others in roles which are fuelled by creativity.

They are quick to learn and adapt to new situations.

Introverted Sensing (Si)

This function encourages archiving past data and details. Introverted Sensing is about trusting one's personal experiences and incidents witnessed in the past to compare and contrast with new experiences. They keep their beliefs and practices intact and are happy to follow the familiar, making them less accessible to the unknown.

Extroverted Sensing (Se)

Extroverted Sensing is the function that makes people aware of and act on their current external experiences to produce desired results. This function is largely driven by one's environment, aesthetics, tastes, etc. which stimulates the physical senses. It also facilitates good observation and response by living and experiencing the physical world.

Introverted Thinking (Ti)

Introverted Thinking occurs when people contemplate actions based on their logical thinking, which assists in taking thoughtful decisions and judgments. This function helps in the systematic analysis of thoughts and deriving action plans based on their set values. In a healthy environment, introverted thinkers are ready to accept different views even though they usually stand for what they comprehend as accurate.

Extroverted Thinking (Te)

Extroverted thinkers automatically bring structure to planning, organizing, and execution activities. They are strong in the organization of data as inputs for works and are good in rational and data-based decisions.

This function can assist them to optimize any process to make it more efficient. A developed Te function makes a system sustainable and empowers it with a long-term vision.

Introverted Feeling (Fi)

Introverted Feeling is the function that brings authenticity to a person since this function deals with morals and what the person truly believes. This function makes people value their existence, life, and values. Value-based thinking with their sets of beliefs can be the driver of their actions.

A developed Fi will evaluate all questions about their beliefs and will upgrade their level of understanding.

Extroverted Feeling (Fe)

Extroverted Feeling aids people to put in efforts to ensure harmony in social groups they belong to, where they are usually found to be actively spreading joy. Personality types with this function, whether in a dominant or assisting mode, will consciously work towards making people happy, sometimes to their personal detriment, all because they need to feel good about themselves.

Cognitive Shadow Functions of MBTI Personality Types

Shadow functions are the opposite of primary functions. The Primary Extraverted & Introverted functions are flipped around to become shadow functions. It will come into play only when one's ego is under threat.

Type	Shadow Cognitive Functions			
	Opposing	Cynical	Deceiving	Immobilizing
ISTJ	Se	Ti	Fe	Ni
ISFJ	Se	Fi	Te	Ni
INFJ	Ne	Fi	Te	Si
INTJ	Ne	Ti	Fe	Si
ISTP	Te	Si	Ne	Fi
ISFP	Fe	Si	Ne	Ti
INFP	Fe	Ni	Se	Ti
INTP	Te	Ni	Se	Fi
ESTP	Si	Te	Fi	Ne
ESFP	Si	Fe	Ti	Ne
ENFP	Ni	Fe	Ti	Se
ENTP	Ni	Te	Fi	Se
ESTJ	Ti	Se	Ni	Fe
ESFJ	Fi	Se	Ni	Te
ENFJ	Fi	Ne	Si	Te
ENTJ	Ti	Ne	Si	Fe

The Behaviour of Cognitive Shadow Function

Introverted Intuition (Ni)

During stress, Ni has to deal with confusion about perspectives and will find themselves in a dilemma to arrive at the right conclusion. This function drives one to be fearful of results and also leads them to doubt their noble decisions, primarily due to overthinking about several possibilities.

Extroverted Intuition (Ne)

This function under strain, will lead to the incorrect use of concepts without factual data and hence forces people to struggle while selecting and finalizing their course of action. Powered with an urge to avoid conflicts, this function pushes people to take actions based on their logic though it proves to be insensitive to others.

Introverted Sensing (Si)

Si function keeps people in their comfort zones as they tend to lean heavily on their past experiences and decisions, making them rigid. They tend to remain closed to new ideas in a stressed scenario.

Extroverted Sensing (Se)

Se personalities, in unhealthy scenarios, have to deal with excessive physical indulgences and compromises. Their actions will not consider long-term consequences, i.e, how their actions affect themselves or others.

Introverted Thinking (Ti)

This function in a stressed environment is characterized by their demand for logical consistency and unwillingness to lose an argument, holding hard onto and safeguarding their position.

Extroverted Thinking (Te)

The Extroverted function in a stressed environment will lead to immediate goal-focused behaviors with a pseudo feeling of order or a false notion of permanency in systemizing. This function brings on a lack of responsibility with regard to actions towards people, the environment, or resources.

Introverted Feeling (Fi)

This function makes people stand by what's perceived by them as a right without the willingness to consider varied views, leaving very little chance of working out a harmonious situation.

Extroverted Feeling (Fe)

During conflicts, Fe function makes people shut down completely to avoid further discussions and will become cold and non-responsive to others, hampering the harmony.

They are eager to protect them during such situations. True to themselves, they are less concerned to cater to others' feelings and expectations.

CHAPTER SUMMARY

1.   All personalities have opposite reactions under normal and stressful environments. Primary cognitive functions appear in normal situations while a combination of shadow cognitive functions appears in stressed situations.

2.   Knowing our default cognitive functions will help bring out our best. The awareness of shadow functions in our personality type will help us make conscious choices and informed decisions about our behavior.

3.   Awareness of unique cognitive functions of personality types brings better understanding and management of situations.

3. INFJ Primary Experiences

**"In a gentle way, you can shake the world"-
Mahatma Gandhi**

INFJs are the Introverted(**I**), Intuitive(**N**), Feeler(**F**), and Judging(**J**) types. In a healthy environment, INFJ exhibits the following cognitive primary functions: Introverted Intuition, Extroverted Feeling, Introverted Thinking & Extraverted Sensing.

An INFJs reaction to any situation will be a combination of these cognitive functions which I will illustrate in the subsequent pages with my experiences with the Primary Cognitive Functions.

INFJ Primary Cognitive Functions	
Leading	Ni
Assistant	Fe
Relief	Ti
Ambitious	Se

Experience with Primary Cognitive Functions

Introverted Intuition

Introverted Intuition (Ni) is the primary function of INFJ. Ni attribute highlights the fact-finding meaning in my work and the want to create a larger impact through my work or role is what drives me. My sense of idealism and my never-ending search for the ideal job or ideas was tiring.

Routine roles failed to excite me, probably as I felt I was not able to make any direct impact in such roles. Hence, it was challenging for me to fit into a framework, and I found myself approaching my employers to expand my work roles.

I felt a need to add to my working knowledge and strengthen my profile with certifications and was thus motivated to update myself on the subject of sustainability. Ni aroused in me a strong sense of empathy and thus ignited the urge to spread awareness in my social circle of the unavoidable climatic catastrophes, waiting to happen. I became a strong advocate for environmental protection and sustainable living in my social groups. My home had undergone a change in line with a more sustainable approach to living. My interest in gardening quipped and I joined peer groups to keep my fire going.

I recall that I used to stress the importance of reskilling oneself and used to push my circle of friends and acquaintances to explore areas of unlearning and relearning. To my surprise, I found that my efforts were not in vain when COVID-19 brought our lives to a standstill. The resultant mass loss of jobs and the revelation of the irrelevance of certain work roles automatically stuck in my mind, being that I had recently dropped hints in my social chats for the need to reskill to remain relevant.

The Ni function also dispenses immense courage in critical situations- In situations when control is nil with a zero chance to fight, what remains is a complete acceptance of the situation. One such instance was accepting my father's demise with complete courage, in the wake of days of warnings of the inevitable happening. I had a strong intuition that I needed to be with my family within the next 2 weeks. Rightly so, in exactly two weeks I was there with my family attending my father's funeral.

Introverted Intuition becomes the primary function of INFJs and INTJs. Association of INTJs brings assurance, as they are a console and guide for INFJs.

Extroverted Feeling

Extraverted Feeling, my assisting and dominant extraverted functions became evident when I started interacting with my social groups on WhatsApp.

This function often has one misunderstood as being an extrovert because of the compelling urge to express ourselves. True to the urges of my personality, I found wielding the pen came naturally to me.

Furthermore, I was a peacekeeper and posted messages of harmony on my social groups. Writing came automatically to me and I was able to manage a good flow of words especially ones of persuasion. My literary support was for varied subjects' environmental protection, health, and to aid and abet the underprivileged. Since my stand was mainly for a common cause, there were hardly any conflicts of interest and I enjoyed a prolonged and unopposed position in my groups. As one of the more active members in my social groups, I expressed my opinions freely and it was well-received.

As an introvert and a feeler, at times I had trouble getting along with groups for a longer period of time, for the want of introverting (to energize me), at the same time I had a strong urge to express my thoughts.

My younger self had an interest in poetry and it was another channel of expression in my capacity as a feeler. I also dabbed in drawing cartoons and music to explore my creativity.

Extroverted Feeling is the Primary Function of ESFJ and ENFJ. These types are a mature comradeship for harmonious co-existence for INFJs.

Introverted Thinking

Introverted Thinking, my relief function, help me balance my extroverted Feeling (Fe) function. This makes me a feeler among thinkers and a thinker among feelers.

This function ignites the practical side in me on an idealistic front, pushing me towards more action. My intuitiveness keeps me in the Ti-Ni loop which helps me decide what task is worth being done, which turns out to be practical for me and valuable to those around me. There was a constant need in me to gather information, to develop myself to add value to others' lives, and to contribute to society.

As support to my habit of exploring various courses and possibilities, my thinking function relieved me of the constant procrastination and explorations of further possibilities, and to look onto a viable career counseling role. Ti gives structure to Ni logically.

Introverted Thinking is the primary function of INTP and ISTP. Their presence gives an INFJ a logical consistency for their intellectual ideas.

Extraverted Sensing

Extraverted Sensing (Es) becomes the ambitious function of an INFJ. The Es function in me enjoys the company of Leading Extraverted Sensor-type personalities who aspire to live to enjoy the moment, rooting for actions that bring a satisfying experience with it.

The Extroverted Feeling combined with the Ni empathy, makes INFJs overdo things frequently. We struggle to maintain boundaries which often leads to a forced correction later on as our personality develops. INFJs make boundaries too rigid or too percolated. To build a healthy boundary, an INFJ has to consciously work on it.

Extraverted sensing, an ambitious function in me, has very little capability for mature handling of state of affairs compared to an Extraverted Sensor in a dominant function. Retaining boundaries is extremely hard and we struggle to find out the extent to which to have fun because there is hardly any limit to the Fe function which is partial to harmony and happiness kicking in.

I enjoy the Se function to the core, by becoming both a fun person among close friends and a sarcastic to those who judge me for being me. It becomes overwhelming and exhausting for me eventually, which makes it essential to take a break from all social life for a much-needed recharge of batteries, while the Dominant Extrovert Sensor gets recharged just by being among people. My previously mentioned series of experiences of quitting social groups and events led to multiple misunderstandings among friends. But Fe's dominance in our personalities makes us honest enough to admit our vulnerabilities and stay in harmony. Extraverted Sensing is the primary function of ESFP and ESTP. They give reminder to INFJs to take care of themselves and to live in the moment.

CHAPTER SUMMARY

1.   INFJs intuitions allow them to read patterns and anticipate incidents, which make them eager to bring awareness to people around them.

2.   INFJs are called Extraverted Introverts or Ambiverts since they need time to themselves and stay away from social circles due to which they are usually misunderstood.

3.   INFJs are social chameleons. Since they can absorb the vibes of people around them, they can adjust to all personality types. They promote harmony in groups.

4.   INFJs are thinkers among feelers and feelers among thinkers. They go through a Ti-Ni loop before making decisions.

5.   The function Fe combined with Se brings out a temporary excessive behavior in INFJs within a small group especially in scenarios where they express themselves in writing.

4. INFJ Shadow Experiences

Never deprive someone of hope; it may be all they have"-

Adolf Hitler

We are now aware that cognitive shadow functions appear usually in a stressed environment and in the case of an INFJ, these cognitive functions create categories such as Extraverted Intuition, Introverted Feeling, Extraverted Thinking, and Introverted Sensing, all in a negative perspective.

INFJ Cognitive Shadow Functions

The shadow functions that play in a stressed environment are tabled as below:

INFJ Shadow Cognitive Functions	
Opposing	Ne
Cynical	Fi
Deceiving	Te
Immobilizing	Si

46

My Experiences with Shadow Cognitive Functions

During stress, conflict, or in an unhealthy situation for an INFJ, their shadow function unfurls unconsciously. As an INFJ, I would like to share with you how my shadow functions behave.

Extroverted Intuition

Extroverted Intuition act as an opposing function for INFJ, creates confusion for the individual concerning the conclusions they make on their intuition. One is pushed to explore multiple possibilities which leads to the rejection of the initial idea, making it extremely impossible to reach a decision.

A person at this point of time is entirely confused about their actions and will be non-decisive, causing them to be numb or to shut down when faced with a crisis where an action is required.

At times such a personality behavior creates an awkward feeling for those around them as they are often perceived as unsure/incompetent especially in a leadership role.

This situation may arise also due to an information overload and the time required for such persons to construct meaning from the current network of data often referred to as the Ni-Ti loop. Ni is the knowing /perspective function and Ti here refers to searching for logical consistency for validating the Ni.

My experience with shadow Extroverted Intuition once occurred while I was participating with a team in a hackathon. I had proposed an idea for the presentation which the team agreed was a well-thought solution and so the business plan discussed was unanimously agreed upon for the presentation.

During our brainstorming for the details of the presentation, I was considering possible alternatives for the presentation model, possible criticisms, and various other criteria which led me to be less than convinced about the plan my team was considering to present.

The information overload did not assist to relieve me of my doubts.

My hesitation to go all the way was noticed by the team and I wanted to justify my concerns, however, time was of the essence, and we were almost about to commence the presentation.

As a result, my team members took charge and completed the presentation slides as per plan. Such a dilemma mostly occurs in situations where we can exercise control. In this scenario, it was too late for corrections, and as the person who initially proposed the presenting idea, I couldn't ask them to take a U-turn on such short notice and so we went ahead and presented the slides even though I felt it was not a viable business plan. The team presentation was rejected but later we registered a viable solution, incorporating the corrections.

Extroverted Intuition is the primary function of ENFP and ENTP. During Stress, Company of them gives an INFJ Clarity of thought and direction for action.

Introverted Feeling

Introverted Feeling functions as a cynic, critical of the harmonious nature of an INFJ. This occurs in situations of abuse, cheating, or manipulation. As natural givers, with high intuition, INFJs are also wary of deceit and the selfish intentions of the people around them.

The instant their senses are alerted, they consciously anticipate the moves of others in the picture and equip themselves with options for reactions.

They tend to avoid conflicts to protect themselves from hurt and intentionally walk away from the zone of conflict without concern for those who are left behind.

This is known as the INFJ 'door slam'. This function also reflects a 'being nice' persona to others, as well as embellishing such personalities with a sense of power that they are the ones in control of a situation, which at times lead people to view INFJs as 'being cold' in these situations.

The introverted cynic in me has responded to instances of abuse and manipulation. Be it, with family or friends, it is an unpleasant sensation for INFJs to hurt anyone with words as we are aware of the hurt caused by such action. Thanks to this sense of empathy, the best strategy we adopt is to stay away from those who cannot respect us and our boundaries.

This strategy though disrupts harmony in relations, is inevitable to avoid conflicts from escalating and to preserve our inner peace. Sometimes INFJs shuts down contacts with people whom they think have manipulated them.

Staying away by severing social connections can be seen as a powerful strategy to escape hurt and regain as a powerful strategy to escape hurt and regain control.

A healthy INFJ in this scenario will be open to considering others' viewpoints and maintaining harmonious social bonds.

Introverted Feeling is the primary function of ISFP and INFP. Their companionship teaches an INFJ, how to be authentic to their feeling by not hampering others' sensibilities.

Extraverted Thinking

Extraverted Thinking is the deceiver function of an INFJ. Since they tend to see the larger picture, during stress, they take details for granted on account of having a larger system to take care of.

This puts them in a helpless situation as their presence of mind is lost in times of stress, and the structured value-based approach is lost. This can lead to messed up actions on their part which can cost those who are dependent on an INFJ's accuracy with details.

They let go of their responsibility to others in such situations, by shifting their focus to themselves while blaming others for the situation they find themselves in, for their incapability and incompetence.

It is here that the seed of vengeance in INFJ sprouts especially when there are bitter experiences such as instances of oppression, discrimination, and prolonged unfairness that they have had to face.

The deceiver function of extraverted thinking once had me pass incorrect information to my boss during a meeting where I had to interpret a drawing dimension.

I couldn't glean sufficient details as I had limited access to and time to study the document while the client was adding to the already stressed environment.

I had the nagging thought that I was passing on unverified information, however, I didn't make the effort to correct it.

The company I worked with employed multiple nationalities and certain company practices leaned towards demarcation and discrimination between the nationalities.

Though I do not usually allow carelessness to reflect in my work and though I am forthright enough to admit shortcomings from my side, at that point of time, I chose to lie, confident in the fact that the error would be taken care of automatically hereafter during further levels of scrutiny.

Extraverted Thinking is the primary function of ENTJs and ESTJs. An INFJ benefits from the company of these types in the systemization of their ideas towards effective implementation.

Introverted Sensing

Introverted Sensing is the immobilizer of the INFJ personality. This function brings rigidity and resentment towards oneself during stress.

INFJs tend to be over-critical about themselves and try to maneuver through the information they have and through their experiences to take rigid decisions for themselves even though such decisions lead them through physical and mental hurt. Such rigid decisions could range from denying oneself of luxuries to an intentional lack of self-care, anchoring such actions to an internal value, or seeing such actions as the right thing to do.

My decision to strictly limit my food consumption was an experience in my shadow function of introverted sensing.

Rather than choosing over-consumption, under-consumption was my response to this shadow function. However, I had to be constantly reminded by my family regarding my health care.

Introverted Sensing is the Primary Function of ISFJs and ISTJs. These types provide an INFJ stability and confidence via practical suggestions.

CHAPTER SUMMARY

1)   During stress, clarity of thought becomes difficult for an INFJ as they get opposing notions about the options under their consideration.

2)   INFJ's usually avoid conflicts and one of the techniques they adopt is to walk away from such situations. This is usually known as the INFJ Door Slam.

3)   INFJ's during stress, prefer taking the easy way out without considering long-term implications.

4)   An unhealthy INFJ adopts a reckless treatment of themselves without deliberating on any future impact.

5. Rare Personality Types & Growth

"As far as we can discern, the sole purpose of human existence is to kindle a light in the darkness of mere being"- Carl Jung

As we discerned in the previous chapters, the cognitive functions of all personality types are unique. If certain types are found less in numbers in society, these types are perceived as being different and are usually isolated in society.

The Rare personality types as per MBTI Manual which fall below 4% in the World Population are as follows.

MBTI RARE TYPE	FREQUENCY IN POPULATION (%)
INTP	3.3
ENTP	3.2
ENFJ	2.5
INTJ	2.1
ENTJ	1.8
INFJ	1.5

The above tabulation indicates that apart from INFJs, which are one of the rarest personality types, ENTJs, INTJs, ENFJs, ENTPs, and INTPs, also fall into the very less frequent types. These types are most likely to find themselves different from the norm, trying to change themselves in an attempt to appear similar to the more common personality types around them, without being aware of the likelihood of other individuals sharing this unique personality type, strengths, and growth path.

MBTI Type Growth

The opportunity for growth of any personality type is dependent on the auxiliary function of that personality type.

The Dominant (Leading) & Auxiliary (Assistant) Functions make up the middle two alphabets of the 4-letter personality type as we have previously seen are called functional pairs.

Extraverts use their dominant function in the outer world and the auxiliary function in their inner world. Since the outer world is of more importance to an extrovert, the development of auxiliary function helps them to contemplate. While for introverts, the dominant function is used for their inner world, the auxiliary function should be developed to balance actions in their outer world.

Personality Development is fulfilled only if the auxiliary function is developed well to support the dominant function. We have seen the Dominant and Auxiliary

(Leading & Assisting) functions of all personality types in Chapter 2.

RARE PERSONALITY GROWTH POTENTIAL FUNCTIONS

TYPE	Leading (Dominant)	Assistant (Auxiliary)	Growth Potential Function
INFJ	Ni	Fe	Extraverted Feeling
INTJ	Ni	Te	Extraverted Thinking
INTP	Ti	Ne	Extraverted Intuition
ENTP	Ne	Ti	Introverted Thinking
ENFJ	Fe	Ni	Introverted Intuition
ENTJ	Te	Ni	Introverted Intuition

Here are a few ways to consider responding to all cognitive growth functions for a holistic personality growth.

- ❖ **Introverted Intuition (Ni) -** Record patterns and utilize them for logical thinking

- ❖ **Extroverted Intuition (Ne) -** Be optimistic, discover and learn new possibilities

- ❖ **Introverted Sensing (Si) -** Make room for novelty, review known facts & traditions

- ❖ **Extroverted Sensing (Se) -** Bringing awareness to activities and interests.

- ❖ **Introverted Thinking (Ti) -** Contemplate the viewpoints of others, even in the belief that only yours is accurate.

- ❖ **Extroverted Thinking (Te) -** Develop traits such as resilience and willpower in order to arrive at sustainable decisions

- ❖ **Introverted Feeling (Fi) -** Act with integrity and take decisions based on personal values.

- ❖ **Extroverted Feeling (Fe) -** Acknowledge conflict. Stir up the courage to resolve conflicts and maintain harmony.

From an INFJ perspective, the Dominant Function is Introverted Intuition (Ni) and the Auxiliary is Extroverted Feeling (Fe).

Below is an illustration of how the growth path for an INFJ would look like.

INFJ Strengths

INFJs are naturals at making people feel comfortable with their warm nature and ready support.

They handle relationships with sincerity; are good listeners and exercise a strong sense of empathy. They are honest and have a way with words; are punctual and respect others' time and space. They need to nurture themselves intellectually to be of value to others, simultaneously pushing people to reach their full potential.

They protect themselves by shutting out people who are abusive and are of a closed mind. Their empathetic stand towards others makes them protective of people and they use both intuition and logic to maintain justice and truth in all situations.

INFJ can be rebels when asked to follow traditions and are usually in search of the deeper meaning in every situation, making them more spiritual than religious. They tend to go along with traditions and customs to preserve harmony.

INFJ Weakness

However, INFJ has weaker sides as well just like any other personality type. They are perceived as arrogant as they refuse to fit in with the general rules of a group and can sometimes adopt extreme behaviors.

They can be bossy at times though they may lack the ground tactics when compared to their dominant Sensing counterparts.

INFJs are less practical as they are idealists and are not willing to be in just any job.

They prefer to walk away from conflicts, rather than handle issues that need to be sorted out. INFJs are known to take abrupt breaks from their social interactions, leaving people wondering about their intent.

They keep pushing themselves and others towards excellence leading to burnouts and over-protectiveness. INFJs have a tendency to overdo things in their urge to maintain happiness and harmony and eventually they burn out. Keeping healthy boundaries is very difficult for INFJs and hence this is an area for improvement.

They are angered when their core values are violated when there is a lack of empathy and in the face of rudeness. Hypocrisy and lies fuel their fire to challenge systems and reveal the truth.

INFJ Growth

The growth potential of Extraverted Feeling is where an INFJ can tap the benefit of evolving their personality type.

Practicing healthy personal and professional boundaries become most essential for INFJs to express themselves to the world. INFJs can deploy their strengths and grow past their shadow functions in various ways. A mature INFJ can be developing their coping skills with fellow personality types and can work on their functions, to make it most effective to them and others.

An evolved INFJ will be confident enough not to hide their identity and will be able to help themselves and the world by utilizing their skills. They will choose to be less of a perfectionist, will be more open to accepting other viewpoints, and will be composed. They will consciously bring change to their excessive sensory behaviors and will take care of their health and wellbeing. They will focus their energies towards more compassionate areas.

Strengths, weaknesses, and the growth path are defined for all personality types. It is up to each personality type to discover a growth path suitable for them.

There are resources like personalityhacker.com and 16personalities.com which give in-depth insights on each personality type. It is strongly recommended to explore one's personality type in-depth to know what it takes for a transformation. One should know what / who they are before looking for what they want to do in life.

The Role of Intuition in Rare Personality types

For all the rare personality types considered in this book, Intuition becomes their natural preference in their functional pair. They are either intuitive thinkers or intuitive feelers.

Intuition is the ability to understand something without the need to think, or to know the facts. It's an access to unconscious cognition, knowledge, insight, or pattern recognition, without any need of conscious reasoning. Israeli psychologist and Nobel prize winner economist Daniel Kahneman is of the opinion that "intelligence is not only the ability to reason but also finding the relevant material in memory and to deploy the attention when needed". He defines intuition as nothing more or less than recognition. So, intuition is helping the intelligence of an intuitive person, with finding the relevant material in memory. The Deployment of attention to the memory when needed, combined with data and facts will help in their ability to reason, which will lead to an intelligent outcome or a decision.

In his book, thinking fast and slow, Daniel Kahneman is giving sufficient caution to intuitive people regarding the use of their intuition.

He says intuition cannot be taken at face value especially in absence of stable regularities. He mentions that people think with their body not with their brain and hence If someone is unhappy or uncomfortable, they lose touch with intuition.

He points out the need for correction in intuitive predictions as they are not regressive and therefore are biased. Many People become overconfident and are prone to place too much faith in their intuitions, without critically considering it, especially when they are impulsive, impatient, and are keen to receive immediate gratification.

Daniel Kahneman has two tips for the intuitive people for the best outcomes of decision i.e., Delay the intuition and be systematic with collecting data.

An article in Forbes suggests reducing stress, meditating, and seeking to imagine and observe future scenarios to cultivate *being more in touch with our intuition. But as Carl Jung says, "Intuition doesn't say what things mean but sniffs out their possibilities. Meaning is given by thinking".*

Famous INFJ Personality Quotes

Some of the popular INFJ Personalities include Artists, Leaders, Psychologists, and Writers. Below are motivational quotes from some famous personalities:

Who looks outside, dreams; who looks inside, awakes.

Carl Jung

We gain strength and courage, and confidence by each experience in which we stop to look fear in the face. We must do that which we think we cannot

Eleanor Roosevelt

Everyone thinks of changing the world, but no one thinks of changing himself

Leo Tolstoy

Unlike any other creature on this planet, humans can learn and understand, without having experienced it. They can think of themselves in other people's places. We do not need magic to change the world, we carry all the power we need inside ourselves already: we have the power to imagine better

J.K. Rowling

Were there none who were discontented with what they have, the world would never reach anything better.

Florence Nightingale

The least I can do is speak out for those who cannot speak for themselves.

Jane Goodall

I think of life itself now as a wonderful play that I've written for myself, and so my purpose is to have the utmost fun playing my part.

Shirley MacLaine

Happiness is as a butterfly which, when pursued, is always beyond our grasp, but which if you will sit down quietly, may alight upon you.

Nathaniel Hawthorne

People respond in accordance to how you relate to them. If you approach them based on violence, that's how they'll react. But if you say, 'We want peace, we want stability,' we can then do a lot of things that will contribute towards the progress of our society.

Nelson Mandela

Love is the only force capable of transforming an enemy into a friend.

Martin Luther King, Jr.

Famous INTJ Personality Quotes

1. *Every deep thinker is more afraid of being understood than of being misunderstood.*

Friedrich Nietzsche

2. *If you don't get out there and define yourself, you'll be quickly and inaccurately defined by others.*

Michelle Obama

3. *When something is important enough, you do it even if the odds are not in your favour.*

Elon Musk

4. *Either you die a hero or live long enough to see yourself become a villain.*

Christopher Nolan

5. *It's better to be hanged for loyalty than rewarded for betrayal*

Vladimir Putin

Famous ENTJ Personality Quotes

1. *Have the courage to follow your heart and intuition. They somehow already know what you truly want to become. Everything else is secondary.*

Steve Jobs

2.   *Don't take it personally. Just take it seriously.*

Gordon Ramsay

3.   *If you just set out to be liked, you will be prepared to compromise on anything at any time and would achieve nothing.*

Margaret Thatcher

4.   *The test of our progress is not whether we add more to the abundance of those who have much; it is whether we provide enough for those who have too little.*

Franklin D Roosevelt

5.   *You are ready and able to do beautiful things in this world, and as you walk through those doors today, you will only have two choices: love or fear. Choose love, and don't ever let fear turn you against your playful heart.*

Jim Carrey

Famous ENFJ Personality Quotes

1. *The best way to not feel hopeless is to get up and do something. Don't wait for good things to happen to you. If you go out and make some good things happen, you will fill the world with hope, you will fill yourself with hope.*

Barack Obama

2. *I've come to believe that each of us has a personal calling that's as unique as a fingerprint - and that the best way to succeed is to discover what you love and then find a way to offer it to others in the form of service, working hard, and also allowing the energy of the universe to lead you.*

Oprah Winfrey

3. *There is nothing like a challenge to bring out the best in man.*

Sean Connery

4. *Courage is the most important of all the virtues because, without courage, you can't practice any other virtue consistently.*

Maya Angelou

5. *We were scared, but our fear was not as strong as our courage.*

Malala Yousafzai

Famous INTP Personality Quotes

1. *Your most unhappy customers are your greatest source of learning.*

Bill Gates

2. *We deserve to experience love fully, equally, without shame, and without compromise*

Elliot Page

3. *I am enough of an artist to draw freely upon my imagination. Imagination is more important than knowledge. Knowledge is limited. Imagination encircles the world.*

Albert Einstein

4. *We cannot allow our public schools to remain in such bad shape and then wonder why we are having so many social problems.*

Stanley Crouch

5. *Truth is ever to be found in the simplicity, and not in the multiplicity and confusion of things.*

Issac Newton

Famous ENTP Personality Quotes

1.   *Failure is always an option*

Adam Savage

2.   *No one respects beauty.*

Sarah Silverman

3.   *If you tell the truth, you don't have to remember anything.*

Mark Twain

4.   *If you're funny, if there's something that makes you laugh, then every day's going to be okay.*

Tom Hanks

5.   *When you have exhausted all possibilities, remember this - you haven't.*

Thomas Edison

CHAPTER SUMMARY

1)   Personality Development is fulfilled only if the auxiliary cognitive function is developed well to support the dominant cognitive function of any type.

2)   Every Personality type has to undergo a transformational journey to bring out their best. Knowing strengths & weaknesses will help in personal growth towards self-actualization.

3)   The Growth opportunity of any personality type is also dependent on owning & managing the shadow functions of a personality type.

6. Careers for Your Personality

"Most People think they know what they are good at. They are usually wrong. And yet, a person can perform only from strength"-Peter Drucker

Lynda Mullaly states quite simply *"Everyone is smart in different ways. But if you judge a fish on its ability to climb a tree, it will spend its whole life thinking that it is stupid".*

Personality is a reflection of a person's innate and nurtured behavior traits. The way a person approaches any situation in life varies according to their inborn abilities. A personality is defined as the most preferred and unconscious way of reacting in an otherwise natural situation. We all have a spectrum of such cognitive functions in us which are set to a frequency of broadcasting that makes us relevant or fit for specific jobs. A career is a combination of value propositions over a period of time and the transition to a least effort work profile, supported by a unique personal skill set, interest, and aptitude along with the right market opportunity. One's very first job need not turn out to be the ideal job. The quest for the ideal job is a journey one has to plan before hitting the road-- by updating one's skills in accordance with the market opportunities while keeping a clear career path in mind.

As we have seen, all 16 personality types have a unique set of cognitive functions and so the resultant combination of responses will vary with each personality. The natural talent and strength each personality possesses when responding to job roles will differ. Certain career streams are deemed suitable for each personality type, in which they are found to usually excel.

Let us see what are the career inclinations for each personality type.

Functional Pairs & Careers

16Personalities.com classifies personalities into 4 groups namely, Analysts, Diplomats, Sentinels, and Explorers. A career choice with vibes resonating close to one's personality traits is a sure path to success because that is where one can use one's natural strength unbounded.

The Myers-Briggs Organization classifies functional pair strengths with their ideal careers.

Let us discover the possibilities.

ST – Sensing and Thinking

Personalities with this functional pair approach work in an objective and analytical manner, focusing on realities. They are good in careers that require a technical approach, compared to growth & development careers.

SF – Sensing and Feeling

Types with the SF functional pair prefer a warm, reality-based, and hands-on career. They are found to excel in jobs requiring a sympathetic approach over jobs requiring an analytical & impersonal approach.

NT- Intuitive & Thinking

NT pair types approach work objectively and analytically, with a focus on those possibilities requiring a technical application. Jobs which require a warm, hands-on, and sympathetic approach will not be suitable for these types.

NF- Intuitive & Feeling.

This pair type embrace life in a warm and enthusiastic manner, focusing on people-centric career possibilities, and are less interested in roles that are impersonal, technical, and factual in nature.

Business Insider in one of its publications listed the top five careers compatible with each personality preference, taken from the career guide book 'Do What You Are' – by Paul D. Tieger, Barbara Barron & Kelly Tieger. According to them, certain roles are best suited for specific personality types. It means these jobs will be more satisfying and fulfilling to these specific types. Job profiles may undergo an upgrade with the onslaught of technological changes. However, if one has focused interest and the required aptitude, they should confidently take up a work role appropriate to their situation, while considering the below suggestions relevant to their personality types as a long-term perspective.

Let us take a look at the top 5 careers suitable to specific personality types.

Analysts – **NT**-Intuitive & Thinking

MBTI Type	Top 5 Careers
Analysts – NT-Intuitive & Thinking	
INTJ Creative perfectionists prefer to do things their way.	Investment Banker
	Personal Financial Advisor
	Software Developer
	Economist
	Executive
ENTP Enterprising creative people who enjoy new challenges.	Entrepreneur
	Real Estate Developer
	Advertising Creative Director
	Marketing Director
	Politician, Political Consultant
ENTJ Natural leaders who are logical, analytical, and strategic planners.	Executive
	Lawyer
	Market Research Analyst
	Management Consultant
	Venture Capitalist
INTP Independent and creative problem solvers.	Computer Programmer/Software Designer
	Financial Analyst
	Architect
	Professor
	Economist

Diplomats - NF-Intuitive & Feeling

MBTI Type	Top 5 Careers
Diplomats - NF-Intuitive & Feeling	
ENFP Curious and Confident Creative types who see possibilities everywhere.	Journalist Advertising Creative director Consultant Restaurateur Event Planner
ENFJ People lovers who are energetic, articulate and diplomatic	Advertising Executive Public Relations Specialist Corporate Coach/Trainer Sales Manager Employment/HR Specialist
INFP Sensitive idealists motivated by their deeper personal values	Graphic Designer Psychologist/Therapist Writer/Editor Physical Therapist HR Development Trainer
INFJ Thoughtful creative people, driven by firm principles and personal integrity.	Therapist/Counsellor Social Worker HR Diversity Manager Organizational Development Consultant Customer Relations Manager

Sentinels - **ST**-Sensing & thinking and **SF**-Sensing & feeling

MBTI Type	Top 5 Careers
Sentinels - ST-Sensing & thinking	
ISTJ	Auditor
Hard workers who	Accountant
value their	Chief Financial Officer
responsibilities and	Web Development Engineer
commitments	Government Employee
ESTJ	Insurance Sales Agent
Realists who are	Pharmacist
quick to make	Lawyer
practical decisions.	Judge
	Project Manager
Sentinels - SF-Sensing & feeling	
ISFJ	Dentist
Modest and	Elementary School Teacher
determined workers	Librarian
who enjoy helping	Franchise Owner
others	Customer service
	representative
ESFJ	Sales Representative
Gregarious	Nurse/Health worker
traditionalists	Social Worker
motivated to help	PR Account Executive
others	Loan officer

Explorers - **SF**-Sensing & feeling and **ST**-Sensing & thinking

MBTI Type	Top 5 Careers
Explorers - SF-Sensing & feeling	
ESFP	Child Welfare Counsellor
Lively and playful people who value common sense.	Primary Care Physician
	Actor
	Interior Designer
	Environmental Scientist
ISFP	Fashion Designer
Warm and sensitive types who like to help people in tangible ways	Physical Therapist
	Massage Therapist
	Landscape Architect
	Storekeeper
Explorers - ST-Sensing & thinking	
ESTP	Detective
Pragmatists who love the excitement and excel in a crisis	Banker
	Investor
	Entertainment agent
	Sports coach
ISTP	Civil Engineer
Straight forward and honest people who prefer action to conversation	Economist
	Pilot
	Data Communication Analyst
	Emergency Room Physician

Super Data Science Club has classified compatible careers in Data Science for different personality types as shown below.

Compatible Data Science Careers for MBTI Types

1   **ENTJ**: Project Manager, Software Architect

2   **ENFJ**: Web Designer, Web Developer

3   **ENTP**: UX Designer, Graphic Designer

4   **ENFP**: UX Researcher, Front-end Developer, Video Game Developer

5   **ESTJ**: Software Analyst, Technical Program Manager, Database Administrator

6   **ESTP**: Web Developer, Data Analyst, UX Researcher

7   **ESFJ**: Machine Learning Engineer, Data Analyst, Support Specialist

8   **ESFP**: Front-end Developer Video Game Developer

9   **INTJ**: System Analyst, Software Engineer, Project Manager

10   **INFJ**: UX Designer, Data Scientist

11   **INTP**: Computer Programmer, Information Security Analyst

12   **INFP**: Software Engineer, Graphic Designer. UX Designer, Front-end Developer

13   **ISTJ**: Data Analyst, Computer Engineer, Computer Programmer

14   **ISFJ**: Software Engineer, Data Scientist

15   **ISFP**: Web Developer, UX Designer Animator

16   **ISTP**: Software Engineer, Systems Support Specialist

Personality Type and Career Selection:

As we are aware, it is not always possible that one is able to start their careers with specific jobs suiting their personality. Whichever the career, there will always be someone at any point of time, who feels that they don't fit in; this is an understanding that will reinforce their decisions to move on to a more appropriate role in which they can play with their strengths. For the uninitiated, it would be wise to choose their education in such a way that it complements their interest, aptitude, and personality strength. Success depends on the investment in the unique strengths of a person over time.

However, it is not implied that one should stay away from any particular type of industry or hesitate to select certain fields. The intention of the book is to usher in awareness to the reader to be able to pick a role with any industry, more compatible with their personality. A career path requires a long-term plan spanning many life stages, which one can easily tailor-make for oneself, using their acquired strengths. A prior understanding of one's destination will help to select the right educational courses and develop the required skills to eventually acquire the most preferred role.

Choosing a career path also depends on knowing an individual's professional interests and strengths. It is always advisable to take additional tests to identify interests and strengths, as a personality will also have nurtured traits.

Clifton Strength Assessment is a popular test to understand the holistic strength of a personality.

As per Truity, the traits that make one successful irrespective of any personality type includes:

Ambitious - Set Goals and are driven by achievements

Challenging - Doesn't avoid conflict and enjoys debate

Expressive - Quick to share thoughts and feelings

Objective - Take rational decisions, not emotional ones

Energetic - High energy level and keep busy

Conceptual - Interested in the knowing big picture

Prominent - Values Social Status and being in public

Even though the types with the highest earning potential are mentioned as Extroverts, Sensors, Thinkers, and Judgers, there are various factors that influence income. It includes educational qualification, Consistency in jobs, Market scenario and the right industry. Gender is also a criterion when it comes to earning. It's reported that Men earn more irrespective of personality traits and types.

Rare Personality Type Career Preferences

All rare personality types are either intuitive thinkers or intuitive feelers.

Intuitive Thinkers are also called Theorists and Intuitive Feelers are called Empaths. Truity Psychometrics classifies Theorists as Driven Directors (**ENTJ**), Strategic Masterminds (**INTJ**), Inspired Inventors (**ENTP**), and Independent Scientists (**INTP**).

Theorists love it when their work includes elements of innovation and invention. They value intelligence and competence and can point out errors in the thought process and can suggest improvements to a weak explanation. They have an objective approach to life. However, Theorists have to work on their emotional intelligence.

Empaths are classified into Inspiring Guides (**ENFJ**), Compassionate Counsellors (**INFJ**), Expressive Advocates (**ENFP**), and Creative Individualists (**INFP**). ENFPs and **INFPs** are among the common types of empaths. Empaths are at their best when they can improve other people's lives. They value care and compassion and are sensitive to others' viewpoints.

They are tactful in their interactions with others and their approach to life is subjective. Empaths should work on their logical thinking as they tend to confuse emotions with factual data.

The Next book in the Clear Career Inclusive Book Series is - Upgrade as Futuristic Empath.

It is interesting to know that MBTI is used by 80% of Fortune 500 companies during their employee selection process. Some universities encourage students to take up career aptitude tests and also facilitate career support centers for students to explore career paths options they are cut out for.

Career Planning for INFJ

University of Saskatchewan Student Employment and Career Center has detailed career planning profiles for all MBTI Types. Regarding the INFJ profile, the University's career center has given the following description of an INFJ's career exploration.

The factors which give INFJ's Career Satisfaction include:

1)   Use of creativity & imagination

2)   Solution-focused programs and services

3)   A unique expression of their abilities

4)   Work that evokes pride

5)   Control in organizing and processing

6)   Mirroring personal values

7)   Work involving skill development

8)   Opportunity for human interaction

At work, INFJs will usually:

1. Value harmony and integrity

2. Inspire co-workers with ideas

3. Provide creative solutions

4. Work to exceed expectations

5. Be organized at work

6. See the big picture

7. Needs an environment that is efficiently run and which considers the needs of employees.

8. Prefer to work in a quiet atmosphere, fostering independent thought and creativity.

9. Want to finish work before relaxing and hence persona needs may be neglected

INFJ work tendencies with room for improvement include:

1) Stubbornness when others disagree with their ideas.

2) Irritation when ideas don't work out.

3) Including Facts and Details at work.

4) Avoiding Conflicts.

5) Withdrawn when their contributions are not valued.

6) Overwhelmed under pressure.

7) Negatively affected by conflicts.

INFJs as Leaders usually:

1. Create future-focussed goals and strategically lead others towards their achievement.

2. Motivate others by affirming individual contributions

3. Face trouble in objectively correcting subordinates

4. Garner inspiration of individuals by effectively communicating their vision to others.

5. Use their creativity and devotion to influence people

6. Expect individuals to complete their duties.

7.   Use their insights in the personal development of people

INFJs during decision making:

1.   Base a decision on what they value

2.   In-depth reflection that considers all implications of their choice

3.   Time consuming while deciding.

4.   Experience internal conflict while making decisions involving the organization and the people.

5.   Need to review the practical components of each decision.

Further details on INFJ Stress Management and Communication are available on the University of Saskatchewan's website. http://students.usask.ca

My Career Path as an INFJ

Subsequent to my graduation in Civil Engineering and post-graduation in Business Administration, my initial job was with a real estate company as a customer care engineer. The monotonous nature of the job and my need to pursue additional value and advanced skills led me to explore new roles in the company. Though internal audits fascinated me, there was no opportunity to pursue that specific role with my current employer. Ensuing the lack of opportunity, I shifted into a marketing profile with an international construction firm. But the work demands did not allow room to pursue my aspirations.

Further to my search for the ideal job, I was rewarded with an interesting opportunity as an internal auditor in a real estate firm, handling their Quality, Environment, Health & Safety, and Social Accountability management systems.

It was a satisfactorily superior experience for me however on realizing the diminishing levels of my professional contribution without adequate roles to perform, I shifted career tracks and took up an independent consulting assignment to implement management systems.

I was keen to up-skill myself in the area of sustainability, and thus upgraded my understanding of CSR Management & Sustainability Reporting.

This led to my placement as Process & Internal Audits Manager with yet another real estate establishment, where I managed their CSR functions as well.

I came one step closer to attaining my career goal as a sustainability consultant, availing my hard-earned knowledge to contribute towards audits and sustainability reporting. Additionally, I reaped immeasurable experience when designated assignments as a CII Sustainability Assessor.

Post-Covid, I found myself sifting through various careers options where I could add value to lives and thus decided to establish myself as a career counselor. I aimed to generate value while working towards inclusion and jump-started my mission to guide students and aspiring professionals towards finding their right careers.

When I look back at my career path, I see a transition from typical engineering and management roles to a more personality-compatible role where I can maximize my 'NF' functional strength.

Psychology continues to fascinate me as I pour over books and videos about the impact on people if they make an effort to find themselves.

Other Personality Identification Tools

Apart from MBTI, there are many other means by which personalities can be identified and assessed. Even though the methodology used in such tools is yet to be validated scientifically, these are widely used around the world to take advantage of the multifaceted findings revealed about each personality.

Some such common tools include Enneagram, Socionics, Big 5, DISC, and RIASAC. The reference links for these tools are provided in the Resources section.

Each of these tools helps us to comprehend ourselves better. In my experience, Enneagram complements MBTI, as both tests helped me understand my personality and the opportunities for my development from different angles.

CHAPTER SUMMARY

1)   Certain careers are ideal for specific personality types as they will naturally fit into the career requirements. Functional Pair strengths throw light on the ideal career for a personality.

2)   Though the first job need not necessarily turn out to be the ideal one, designing a career path towards an ideal career will lead to personality type growth.

3)   Many well-researched personality identification tools can complement each other and the test results can be used to reinforce career decisions.

Conclusion

We have the luxury of having access to varied and voluminous information around us. Yet, the actual value of it towards the benefit of mankind remains largely untapped. Knowing the personality type we belong to is important as understanding the tendencies associated with it to helps us make conscious decisions. Our character traits may hardly vary from the spectrum of the predicted behaviors of our personality type but we can choose to show resilience during stress and can manage our blind spots by being conscious of ourselves and selecting the auto mode of the healthy side.

Understanding what is ideal for us is not the same for all other types is where our maturity in handling relationships starts. It's a paradigm shift from benchmarking with ourselves to an external point where there is a consensus from all types according to their preferences. Personal transformation helps us to be successful in life as we can utilize our maximum potential, leading to self-actualization. This knowledge has the power to heal relationships also.

The best careers suitable for each person are defined according to each personality type.

An ideal career will be a scientific representation of the demands from that role and the requirements from the executor.

If the natural strength and interests of any personality type are in alignment with a job, it will lead to productivity and job satisfaction. Knowing your right place early on will give you enough time to plan, invest and be successful in your specific area of work. All rare personality types need help with their identification and they deserve to understand their strengths. They should be encouraged to contribute to their fullest potential especially in workplaces, which they will happily and sincerely. The tendency in us to judge people for their 'strange' behaviors needs to be thought through as they might be simply living as what they are and not pretending to be what they are not.

Acceptance and participation of these personality types can be considered a part of the Inclusion & Diversity policy of companies as these kinds often try to fit themselves in roles designed for the majority types.

Assistance for self-growth should be given to people with such characteristics as they usually struggle to find the right place in society. They have the strength to make lasting impacts in the world with their respective strength and companies should be open to considering their representation in the talent pool seeing the rarity of these types.

Every personality type goes through a transformation over time, even though their basic inclinations remain constant. The growth of one's personality becomes refined and the healthy side of the personality receives reinforcement through learning and training.

With the help of the personality tests mentioned in this book, I could relate to myself as an Advocate/Counselor (INFJ), which is what I have become at this point of time in my life even before coming across these tests. Hence, I endorse the accuracy and authenticity of what has been disclosed by these tests, particularly in my case. It is my humble request to view this book as an attempt to enlighten the readers of all MBTI types, especially the rare personality types to support their possibilities for transformation.

Everyone has the power to change the world, by owning their personality and taking necessary steps towards their personal growth. To achieve that, everyone should be open to the science psychology can reveal and should not shy away from the responsibility of leaving imprints for future generations.

About the Author

Devi Sunny is an Author & Founder of Clear Career Inclusive a community with a mission to support inclusion by developing young leaders in work places. She assists in the career development of eligible students and aspiring professionals at Clear Career.

You can connect with her at: contact@clearcareer.in

May I ask for a Review?

Thank you for taking out time to read this book. Reviews are the essential for any author. I look forward to your feedback and reviews for this book. I welcome your inputs to incorporate in and deliver an even better book in my next attempt in the very near future.

Your support will help me to reach out to more people. Thanks for supporting my work. I'd love to see your review and feel free to contact me for any clarifications.

contact@clearcareer.in

Preview of Books

Book 2 <u>Upgrade as Futuristic Empaths</u>

Find your strength to give your best!

Are you an empath? Do you know what an empathy trap is? How can you <u>transform empathy into a strength and build successful careers</u>?

Empaths have intuitive feelings (owing to the <u>cognitive functional pair "NF"</u> in their personality type) as their psychological preference. Personality types <u>ENFP, ENFJ, INFJ, and INFPs are natural empaths</u> as per the **MBTI Personality types** according to www.16personalities.com and www.Truity.com. Empaths are also called **Idealists & Diplomats. Highly Sensitive People** belong to these MBTI types. To face the realities of the world and to be successful in endeavours which have larger impacts, empaths need to embrace practicality and rise above their personality stereotype or one-sidedness.

Dr.Dario Nardi, Author of the book **Neuroscience of Personality**, suggests transcendence or the individuation process, a term coined by **Carl Jung,** the essence of which is to have an integrated personality growth. Empaths have a larger role to play in this world and most of them are underplaying their natural strength.

<u>*By adopting the 5 key steps discussed in this book, anyone, especially empaths can easily find their career paths to success, thereby leaving a positive impact on this world.*</u>

Key Learnings from the book - Upgrading as Futuristic Empaths.

Chapter 1 Understanding Empaths

"Objective judgment, now, at this very moment. Unselfish action, now, at this very moment. Willing acceptance — now, at this very moment — of all external events. That's all you need." - Marcus Aurelius

✓ **Find How!**

Book 3 <u>**Onboard as Inclusive Leaders**</u>

Find Your Potential to Impact the Best!

How Inclusive are you? Are you unconsciously biased?

Do you promote Psychological Safety?

This book will help you find answers and enable you <u>*Onboard as Inclusive Leaders.*</u>

Innovation, financial performance and employee productivity are indispensable for business growth. Inclusion helps in achieving these objectives of business. Diversity in line with inclusion and equity creates a sense of belonging in employees.

This book helps to develop the essential qualities required to be hired as an inclusive leader; ***understand unconscious biases, the importance of psychological safety and how it has an impact on workplace productivity.***

The book also gives you the free test links to understand your MBTI personality type, strength, and Bias Tests (The Implicit Association test - Harvard University)

Key Learnings from the book – Onboard as Inclusive Leaders

Chapter 1 Knowing Inclusion

1. Why do we need Inclusive Leaders?
2. What is an Inclusive Workplace?
3. Features of an Inclusive Workplace
4. Challenges of Inclusive Workplace
5. Merit based Inclusion
6. Who is an inclusive leader?

Chapter 2 Inclusion Gap

1. Facts of Diversity & Inclusion
2. Microaggression
3. Unconscious Bias
4. 16 Unconscious Biases
5. Bias Test (The Implicit Association Test)
6. The Cost of Unconscious Bias

Chapter 3 Inclusion in Practice

1. Inclusion in the workplace
2. Inclusion Strategies at Ingersoll Rand
3. Inclusion Mandate
4. Expectations of Gen Z
5. Disability Inclusion
6. LGBTQ+ Inclusion
7. Six Signature Traits of Inclusive Leaders
8. Risks of Casual Diversity Programs

Chapter 4 Inclusion Participants

1. Types of Inclusion
2. Physical Inclusion
3. Psychological Inclusion
4. Importance of Assertiveness for Empaths at work
5. Empathy and Neuroscience of Personality Types
6. Preparing the Team for Inclusion

Chapter 5 Inclusion Process

1. Inclusion Strategy
2. Psychological safety
3. International Standards for Inclusion Process
4. Inclusive Job Posting
5. Inclusive Hiring
6. DEI Interview Questions
7. Disparate Treatment & Disparate Impact

Chapter 6 Inclusion Measurement

1. Measurement of Inclusion
2. Gartner Inclusion matrix
3. How Inclusive is your leadership?
4. Fundamental Interpersonal Relations Orientation (FIRO®)
5. Empathy & Inclusion Measurement
6. Industry Measurement of Diversity & Inclusion

"If someone can prove me wrong and show me my mistake in any thought or action, I shall gladly change. I seek the truth, which never harmed anyone: the harm is to persist in one's own self-deception and ignorance."
— Marcus Aurelius

We need more inclusive leaders who will consider others in their decisions and that alone can give rise to sustainable development and positive impacts for people and the planet.

✓**Find How?**

Acknowledgement

My gratitude to the readers of my book, for your time and reviews, and to all my well-wishers for your support. I am indebted to all who reached out to me with feedback and input.

I have to start by thanking my family, friends, and classmates for their encouragement, counsel, and good-natured jibes.

Extending my wholehearted gratitude to everyone on the Author Freedom Hub, special thanks to Som Bathla for his vote of confidence and my fellow authors for their unbounded support.

To Anita Jocelyn for her editorial help towards the completion of my book.

I thank my friends and colleagues who helped me with their insights and experiences of their work place inclusion. Your inputs were critical in the completion of this book and helped me gather information to cover this topic in details for my readers.

I am grateful to Mr. Sareej for his efforts towards the beautiful cover design.

In no way at all the least, I am very thankful to my spouse Jo and our son Yakob for helping me out immensely by allowing me space and time to pursue my interests and creating a conducive environment to achieve my goals.

To my mother Prof.Thresiamma Sunny, I am thankful for her unwavering support and inspiration to always deliver my best.

I could not have done it without you all.

References

1. www.weforum.org
   The 3 key skill sets for the workers of 2030 | World Economic Forum (weforum.org)

2. www.personalityhacker.com
   Home — Personality Type and Personal Growth | Personality Hacker

3. https://integrative9.com
   27 Subtypes, Instincts of Claudio Naranjo (integrative9.com)

4. www.socioniks.net
   About us - Official site of the School of Humanitarian Socionics of Viktor Gulenko (socioniks.net)

5. www.personalitymax.com
   An In-depth Explanation of the Eight MBTI Preferences (personalitymax.com)

6. www.goodreads.com
   Isabel Briggs Myers Quotes (Author of 50 Psychology Classics) (page 2 of 3) (goodreads.com)

7. http://www.personalityjunkie.com
   The 8 Jungian Functions: Roles, Images & Characteristics (personalityjunkie.com)

8. http://wellandgood.com
   8 MBTI functions explain how personality tests act in the world | Well+Good (wellandgood.com)

9. http://www.introvertdear.com

The 21 Most Inspirational Quotes by Famous INFJs (introvertdear.com)

10. www.springboard.com
    Best Careers for Your MBTI Personality Type
    (springboard.com)

11. www.myersbriggs.org
    The Myers & Briggs Foundation - Myers and Briggs
    Foundation (myersbriggs.org)

12. www.businessinsider.in
    Here are the best jobs for every personality type |
    BusinessInsider India

13. http://sdsclub.com
    Best Data Science Careers for MBTI Personality
    Type - SDS Club

14. www.typeinmind.com
    THE STACK — Type in Mind

15. http://www.personalityclub.com
    The Complete Introduction to the Shadow
    Functions in MBTI | Personality Club

16. http://students.usask.ca
    INFJ.pdf (usask.ca)

TEST LINKS

1. www.16personalities.com – For the MBTI test
2. www.truity.com – For the Enneagram test
3. www.socioniks.net –For the 16 Sociotype test
4. www.truity.com – Free Big Five Personality test
5. www.truity.com – DISC Assessment Free Personality Test for Business
6. www.truity.com – Holland Code Job Aptitude Test

THE HEALER COUNSELLOR

INFJ

You are warm, caring and insightful into the needs and motivations of others. You are a great listening ear to your friends in need. You want the work in your life to make a difference in others and help others become better.

INTUITIVE	WORK ALONE	AUTHENTIC
INSIGHTFUL	ORGANIZED	EMPATHETIC

FAMOUS INFJs

Carl Jung

Cate Blanchett

Gandhi

TOP CAREERS

Nutritionist
Pastor
Career Consultant
Movie Producer
Artist
Teacher
Author
Counsellor
Welfare Officer
Dramatist

INTROVERSION
You recharge your energy in solitude

INTUITION
You enjoy possibility, theory and big ideas

FEELING
You make values-centered, people oriented decisions

JUDGING
You are organized, preferring to keep a schedule

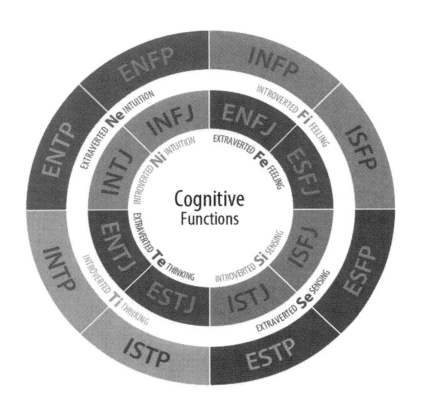

WHAT MAKES EACH COGNITIVE FUNCTION HAPPY

Live Your Best Life

Se — EXPERIENCE

You want to interact fully with your environment and be able to make an impact. Go whitewater rafting. Get in the car and drive without a destination. Immerse yourself in the opportunities, beauty, and thrills available in the present moment.

Si — IMMERSION

As a specialist you enjoy tinkering with your hobbies, mastering a skill and repeating it. You enjoy meaningful routines, rituals, and practices that give you a sense of inner comfort and well-being.

Ne — IDEAS

You want to generate possibilities and innovative new ways of doing things. You enjoy change, risk, novelty, and adventure. You crave freedom and a sense that tomorrow is unknowable.

Ni — MEANING

You want to search for meaning in abstract concepts, philosophies, and symbolism. You see everything in the tangible world as being connected in complex, hidden ways and your goal is to understand those connections. .

Te — ACCOMPLISHMENT

You are energized by meeting objectives, getting things done, and finding the best way to accomplish something. Creating order and efficiency in your environment gives you a lot of joy.

Ti — PRECISION

The search for truth and accuracy guides you. You want to understand the logical processes behind how things work and you want to discard inaccurate or biased thinking from your mind to live with truth and clarity.

Fe — UNITY

Whether you're reading a book or talking with a friend, you get satisfaction from understanding other people's feelings and values. You enjoy working with people to create unity, harmony, and a feeling of shared purpose.

Fi — INDIVIDUALITY

You are energized by getting in touch with your own values, ethics, ideals, and desires. You believe in being true to your feelings and wishes in life, even if that makes you a misfit.

THE
16 PERSONALITY
TYPES
according to Jung,
MBTI & Kersey

I - introvert   T - thinking   N - intuition   P - perceiving
E - extravert   F - feeling   S - sensing   J - judging

Temperament
Role
Role Variant

Sources: K. Jung Psychological Types,
Myers-Briggs Type Indicator (MBTI),
D. Keirsey Temperament Sorter

visualized by Mark and Anna Vital

adioma

Printed in Great Britain
by Amazon

19702788R00066